FLEXIBLE MINDSET

FLEXIBLE MINDSET

PATH TO SUCCESS

VISHAL C RAJPUT

Twitter Id - @OfficialRajputV

Notion Press

Old No. 38, New No. 6
McNichols Road, Chetpet
Chennai - 600 031

First Published by Notion Press 2016

ISBN 978-1-946204-85-1

Contents

Foreword

As the idea of writing this book emerged, I constantly questioned and argued with my father about the purpose of writing it so soon. I felt that it was not the right time to share it. But after much discussion, I now understand that it is very important for the youth to understand the importance of the ratio between failure and success.

You will be reading about the people that are successful today, but who had initially faced rejection and failure. They too were overlooked. The common characteristic shared by all these outstanding personalities is a FLEXIBLE MINDSET. It means they were not stubborn and did not believe in the mindset that was set by the society. They all overcame their situations and easily adapted to the continuously changing situations. Nothing held them back from implementing their ideas that made them successful.

This book is very special to me because the outstanding personalities it discusses helped me overcome my **Existential depression** and kept me inspired.

Beyond everything, this book is about aspiring to do what you believe in and how you can change the situation around you.

Acknowledgements

This book is the synergistic product of my failure and research. Capturing diverse elements has its own set of challenges, as a book essentially has a linear format, is passive by nature and forces the reader to go with the pace of the author.

Within our organization, i.e., my home, my dad Mr Chandrashekhar Rajput incubated the idea of writing this book and supported me with motivation and guidance. I thank my mom Mrs Vaishali C Rajput for guiding me through this entire process and being a support system.

I would like to thank the World Wide Web because a large portion of research that went into writing this book was based on documents provided on the net as well as Indian and foreign media sources. These names mentioned above have helped me out of my depression and shaped my thinking process. If I have inadvertently failed to name the above mentioned legends' honorific titles correctly, then I apologize in advance.

My sincere thanks to everybody at Notion press – from the editors to the marketing department – for helping me publish this book.

Change Your Mindset

The only thing that stands between you and your success is your mindset.

You must have heard people asking you to change your mind-set, but have you ever wondered how to go about doing it?

In this chapter, I will be explaining flexible thinking processes and giving you a glimpse of various other options that will help you achieve a FLEXIBLE MINDSET.

The first and foremost aspect that you have to change is your perspective, i.e., your way of looking at situations in your life.

To understand your thinking process, you need to ask yourself the following questions:

1. How Flexible is my mind?
2. Am I easily adaptable or do I fear change?
3. Do I believe in myself?
4. How well do I work under pressure?
5. Do I take calculated risks?
6. How do I face hurdles?
7. Etc. (n number of questions that you pose to yourself)

One more point that I would like to highlight here is that, "A smart person learns from his own mistakes, while a wise person learns from his own mistakes as well as the mistakes of others."

Elevate your life with optimistic thinking. Keep your mind open to hidden opportunities and keep your eyes focused on your goal.

Motto

Whenever I hear about students committing suicide due to failure in their exams, it hurts me very deeply. The parents of such students go through unbearable pain apart from social stigma.

This is my kind effort to bring positivity in the thinking process of the society. I would like to show how a person can change his/her life by facing failures with a positive attitude. By changing our attitudes, we can elevate not only ourselves but can also be assets to the society. People with positive mindsets are like fruit-bearing trees whereas negative people are like parasites hindering the growth of the society. It is important to educate ourselves about the necessity of a flexible mindset. Even if one percent of my readers are motivated by my thoughts and are able to change unfavorable conditions to favorable conditions just by changing their mindset, I may consider myself successful.

Sometimes,our egos or fears hinder the progression of our ideas or ventures. By shedding our stubborn egos and fears and making our mindsets flexible, unfavorable situations will appear favorable to us.

Bill Gates

'I failed in some subjects in exam, but my friend passed in all. Now he is an engineer in Microsoft and I am the owner of Microsoft.' – Bill Gates

William Henry "Bill" Gates III (born October 28, 1955) is an American business magnate, entrepreneur, philanthropist, investor and programmer. In 1975, Gates and Paul Allen co-founded Microsoft, which became the world's largest PC software company. During his career at Microsoft, Gates held the positions of chairman, CEO and chief software architect and was the largest individual shareholder until May 2014. Gates has authored and co-authored several books.

At age 17, Gates formed a venture with Allen, called Traf-O-Data, to make traffic counters based on the Intel 8008 processor. In early 1973, Bill Gates served as a congressional page in the U.S. House of Representatives.

Gates graduated from Lakeside School in 1973 and was a National Merit Scholar. He scored 1590 out of 1600 on the SAT and enrolled at Harvard College in the autumn of 1973. While at Harvard, he met Steve Ballmer, who would later succeed Gates as CEO of Microsoft.

Gates, of course, is the richest man in the world, topping the Forbes Annual Ranking list sixteen times in the past twenty-one years. But before launching Microsoft, he and Paul Allen were co-owners of a failed business called Traf-O-Data, a computerized machine for processing paper tapes from traffic counters. While the product went belly up, Gates and Allen used what they learned to go on and create the largest software company in the world.

Net worth

0$ to 78.3 billion $

Points to learn from Bill Gates:

1. Manage pressure and overcome your failure.
2. Convert an unfavorable situation into a favorable one. Believe that you can bring a change that will benefit not only you but society as a whole.
3. Think big and aim higher in order to reap more benefits.
4. Be humble despite your success as fruit-bearing branches always hang low.
5. Keep pursuing your dreams.

Dhirubhai Ambani

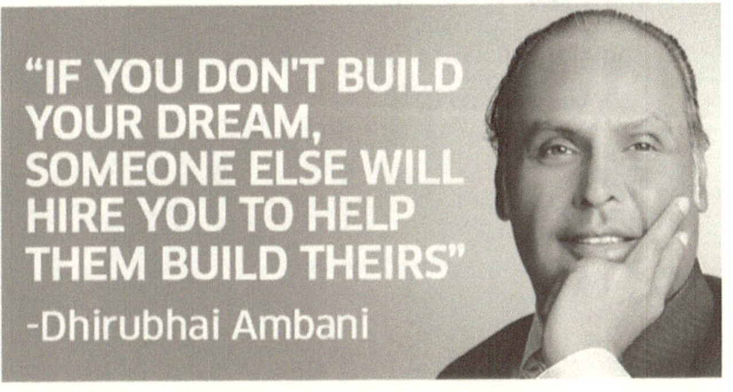

'Think Big, Think Fast, and Think Ahead.
Ideas are no one's monopoly' - Dhirubhai Ambani

DhirajlalHirachand "Dhirubhai" Ambani (28 December 1932 – 6 July 2002) was an Indian business tycoon who founded Reliance in Bombay with his cousin. He was featured in the *The Sunday Times* top 50 businessmen in Asia. Ambani took Reliance Industries public in 1977 and by 2007, the combined fortune of the family was $60 billion, making the Ambanis the third richest family in the world. Ambani died on 6 July 2002. In 2016, he was honored posthumously with the Padma Vibhushan, India's second highest civilian honor, for his contributions towards the field of Trade and Industry.

Dhirubhai was born in India. His father was a school teacher and his family didn't have a lot of money. He traveled with his family to Yemen at the age of sixteen where he started his first job. After some time, Dhirubhai returned to India and founded his first company, but things didn't go well with his partner and the partnership came to an end.

Things to learn from Dhirubhai Ambani's story:

1. Whatever the situation may be, it all depends on how you take it.
2. You don't have to believe in anything else if you believe in yourself.

Dr Subhash Chandra

'Don't kill any idea due to lack of money.'- Dr Subhash Chandra

Subhash Chandra (born **Subhash Chandra Goel** 30 November, 1950) is an Indian media baron with interests in packaging, media lottery and cinema. He is the chairman of Essel Group, an Indian conglomerate. He was the former Chairman of India's TV channel network Zee Media but resigned as Director & Non-Executive Chairman of the Company with effect from May 24, 2016. He has been elected to the RajyaSabha from the Haryana state in the by-elections on 11 June 2016.

Subhash Chandra was born on 30 November 1950. In 1970, while he was studying in the 10th grade, he dropped out of school to join his family business, asa commission agent and trader who procured and supplied rice to the Food Corporation of India. In the 1980s, he started manufacturing flexible packaging (mainly plastic tubes) for toothpaste etc. under the name "Essel Packaging." He followed up with a leisure park called Essel World in North Mumbai. In 1992, he launched Zee Television in collaboration with Li KaShing. He also launched the first online lottery and first Dish TV in India.

If you find his story interesting, read his autobiography titled *The Z Factor.*

Important lessons to learn:

Tweet by Dr Subash Chandra

Losing is indeed a great learning experience. It is the most important lesson you could learn; strengthening you & preparing you to work harder!

He is an optimistic person and a motivational guru who took calculated risks that made him a successful person. He kept his mind open to the opportunities that he came across.

Subashji keeps motivating youngsters through Zee Channel, books and generates positivity in the environment. His contribution towards society will always be our asset and will keep motivating all of us.

And, also watch *Dr Subash Chandra Show* for more motivation.

Sir Richard Branson

"Complexity is your enemy. Any fool can make something complicated. It is hard to keep things simple." –Sir Richard Branson

Sir Richard Charles Nicholas Branson (born 18 July, 1950) is an English business magnate, investor and philanthropist. He is best known as the founder of the Virgin Group, which comprises more than 400 companies.

Branson expressed his desire to become an entrepreneur at a young age. At the age of sixteen, his first business venture was a magazine called *Student*. In 1970, he set up a mail-order record business. In 1972, he opened a chain of record stores, Virgin Records, later known as Virgin Megastores. Branson's

Virgin brand grew rapidly during the 1980s, as he set up Virgin Atlantic and expanded the Virgin Records music label.

In March 2000, Branson was knighted at Buckingham Palace for "services to entrepreneurship." In July 2015, Forbes listed Branson's estimated net worth at US $5.2 billion.

Branson has dyslexia and had poor academic performance as a student and on his last day at school, his headmaster, Robert Drayson, told him he would either end up in prison or become a millionaire. Branson's parents were supportive of his endeavors from an early age.

Key points:

- Parents play a very important role in a child's development.
- Believe in your child as they are your own blood.
- Branson followed his dream of becoming an entrepreneur and made it successful by believing in himself.
- He never let dyslexia or his poor academic performance become obstructions in his path to success. This is an example of a flexible mindset.
- Do not be embarrassed by your failures, learn from them and start again.– Sir Richard Branson

Mahashay Dharampal Gulati

'Take a chance; you never know what life can give you.' – Anonymous

Mahashay Dharampal Gulati was born on 27 March, 1923 in Sialkot (Pakistan). His father Mahashay Chunnilal and mother Mata Chanan Devi were philanthropic and religious followers of AryaSamaj.

In the year 1933, he left school before he completed the fifth grade. In 1937, he set up, with the help of his father, a small business selling mirrors. This was followed by a soap business, a carpentry job; selling clothes, then selling hardware and eventually selling rice. Somehow, these petty businesses could not hold him for long and he again joined hands with his father in his parental business, i.e., selling spices under the name Mahashian Di Hatti, popularly known as 'Deggi Mirch Wale.'

After the partition of the country, he came to India and reached Delhi on 27 September, 1947. At that time he had only Rs1500 with him. Out of this amount, he purchased a tonga for Rs650 and drove it from New Delhi Railway Station to Qutab Road and Karol Bagh to Bara Hindu Rao at two Annas *sawari* for a few days. Thereafter, he bought a small wooden *khokha* (shop) measuring 14ft. x 9 ft. at Ajmal Khan Road, Karol Bagh, New Delhi and started his family business of ground spices and again raised the banner of Mahashian Di Hatti of Sialkot 'Deggi Mirch Wale.' He usedto distribute his spices in the villages of Bihar and Odisha, mainly in Bihar East Singbhum (now in Jharkhand) and Odisha's Mayurbhanj district.

Points to learn:

- Don't be victimized by situations.
- Follow your instincts with an open mind.
- Strive hard and don't be satisfied until your dreams get accomplished.
- Dharampalji is an excellent example of a person with a flexible mindset, as he did not use beautiful models to showcase his product.Instead, he himself is the brand ambassador of his own product.

Henry Ford

"Failure is simply the opportunity to begin again, this time more intelligently." – Henry Ford

These days, Henry Ford is a household name, but it hasn't always been that way. At 23, Ford was just a machinist's apprentice with big aspirations.

A few years later, he was known as an intelligent, yet failed engineer who just couldn't produce. His need to perfect every product he created led to late deliveries to customers and this tarnished his early reputation.

But it was these early failures that taught him valuable lessons and sparked his future success.

His first lesson came when he designed his first automobile, the Quadricycle. There's a good reason why you've probably never heard of the Quadricycle: it wasn't fit for mass-production. But it did get young Henry Ford's name out there, leading him to his first financial backers and his first company: The Detroit Automotive Company.

Detroit Automotive Company had a similar, short-lived history like the Quadricycle. Despite having William H. Murphy, one of the most prominent businessmen of the time as a financial backer, Ford still couldn't get his product fine-tuned enough to sell. Perfectionism got the best of him and after a year and a half of tinkering; he still had nothing to show for his work. Murphy, along with all the stockholders, began to show concern. Soon, the board of directors dissolved and the company disbanded. It was a short-lived project and a failure in the eyes of the industry.

In the bureaucratic automotive industry of the early 1900's, getting a second chance was a rarity. But after reflecting on his failure, Ford contacted Murphy yet again and offered new ideas and solutions to past problems. Murphy gave him a second chance with the condition that he worked with a supervisor. For Ford, being supervised by someone who knew nothing about engineering and design was infuriating and unacceptable. He left his arrangement and decided to try other ways to achieve his dream.

"Failure is simply the opportunity to begin again, this time more intelligently." -Henry Ford

With a tarnished reputation and no financial backers, Ford was in a bad spot. He knew he had to work around the system somehow. After months of looking for an unconventional backer who wouldn't interfere with his design processes, he found the right man - Alexander Malcomson.

He now had the backing he needed to begin creating the automobile he had always envisioned - the Model A. To take care of the distribution and business matters that had plagued Ford in the past, he brought in James J Couzens to be the Vice President of Ford Motor Company.

The first batch of the Model A's were anything but flawless. In fact, they had so many problems that the Ford Motor Company had to send mechanics to every corner of the country to fix cars. But when the mechanics came back, they came back with feedback; feedback that Ford immediately implemented in his assembly line. With the help of Couzens, they kept shipping, kept making mistakes and kept learning.

It would take five more years and countless failures before the Ford Motor Company came out with the world's best automobile - the Model T. The Model T revolutionized the automobile industry and brought Ford to the forefront of the industry.

What's important to note is Ford's perseverance and ability to overcome setbacks. He used failure and the feedback gathered from those failures to fine-tune his design ideas and eventually change the way we get around town.

Show some grit, work hard and soon, your efforts will pay off. They might even drive you into the history books like Henry Ford.

Learning from failure can never be possible if you have a stubborn mindset. It will never ever help you grow. Growth needs freedom of mind to think and accomplish.

Swami Ramdev Baba

"God has made you to accomplish something great.
Don't run! Don't hide!
Those who run are cowardly and weak." – Swami Ramdev

Swami Ramdev was born to Ram Niwas Yadav and Gulabo Devi. He studied Indian scripture, Yoga and Sanskrit in various gurukuls. He became a sanyasi and adopted the name Swami Ramdev. While living in Kalwa Gurukul in Jind district, Haryana, he offered free yoga training to villagers for some time. He then moved to Haridwar in Uttarakhand, where he practiced intense self-discipline and meditation and spent several years studying ancient Indian scriptures at Gurukul Kangri Vishwavidyalaya.

Swami also suffered from paralysis and overcame it by practicing yoga at a very young age.

Swami Ramdev has worked a lot in the area of development and awareness of yoga.

Patanjali Ayurved was started by Baba Ramdev and Acharya Balkrishna ten years ago in Haridwar. As of early-March 2016, the company's turnover has already crossed ₹45 billion (USD670 million) and is cruising at a monthly rate of about ₹5 billion (USD 74 million) to ₹5.5 billion (USD 82 million). And most importantly, all the money is used for human welfare.

Key Points:

Determination can help a person out of any illnesses or bad situations.

Oprah Winfrey

"Surround yourself with people who are going to take you higher." – Oprah Winfrey

Winfrey was born into poverty in rural Mississippi to a teenage single mother and later raised in an inner-city Milwaukee neighborhood. She has stated that she was molested during her childhood and early teens and became pregnant at fourteen; her son died in infancy. Sent to live with the man she calls her father, a barber in Tennessee, Winfrey landed a job in radio while still in high school and began co-anchoring the local evening news at the age of nineteen. Her emotional ad-lib delivery eventually got her transferred to the daytime-talk-show arena, and after boosting a third-rated local Chicago talk show to first place, she launched her own production company and became internationally syndicated.

Oprah has long believed that education is the door to freedom, offering a chance at a brighter future. Through her private charity, The Oprah Winfrey Foundation, she has awarded hundreds of grants to organizations that support the education and empowerment of women, children and families in the United States and around the world. Amongst her various philanthropic contributions, she has donated millions of dollars toward providing a better education for students who have merit but no means. She also created The Oprah Winfrey Scholars Program which gives scholarships to students determined to use their education to give back to their communities in the United States and abroad.

Net worth 3.1 billion USD

Key Point:

Oprah faced lots of unfavorable situations, but she always had a positive attitude towards life. That's what is called being open-minded.

Though she struggled a lot at a very young age, she gave society her positivity, a part of her fortune and knowledge. Whenever you get succession life, give something back to the world; until then your success is useless. If you do not share your success, you will be like a beautiful flower with no fragrance.

"Education is the door to freedom." – Oprah Winfrey

Ellen DeGeneres

"Be Kind to One Another." -Ellen DeGeneres

Ellen Lee DeGeneres (born January 26, 1958) is an American comedian, television host, actress, writer and producer. DeGeneres starred in the popular sitcom *Ellen* from 1994 to 1998 and has hosted her syndicated TV talk show, *The Ellen DeGeneres Show,* since 2003.

DeGeneres was born and raised in Metairie, Louisiana. She is the daughter of Betty DeGeneres (née Elizabeth Jane Pfeffer), a speech therapist and Elliott Everett DeGeneres, an insurance agent. She has one brother, Vance, a musician and producer. She is of French, English, German and Irish descent. She was raised as a Christian Scientist until age thirteen. In 1973, her parents filed for separation and were divorced the following year. Shortly after, Ellen's mother married Roy Gruessendorf, a salesman. Betty Jane and Ellen moved with Gruessendorf from the New Orleans area to Atlanta, Texas. Vance stayed with his father. On a February 2011 episode of her show, she told her studio audience of a letter from the New England Historic Genealogical Society confirming she is the fifteenth cousin to Catherine, Duchess of Cambridge via their shared common ancestor Thomas.

DeGeneres graduated from Atlanta High School in May 1976, after completing her first years of high school at Grace King High School in Metairie, Louisiana. She moved back to New Orleans to attend the University of New Orleans, where she majored in communication studies. After one semester, she left school to do clerical work in a law firm with a cousin, Laura Gillen. Her early jobs included working at J. C. Penney, and being a waitress at T.G.I. Friday's and another restaurant, a house painter, a hostess, and a bartender. She relates much of her childhood and career experiences in her comedic work.

DeGeneres's first regular TV role was in a short-lived Fox sitcom called *Open House.*

In 1992, producers Neal Marlens and Carol Black cast DeGeneres in their sitcom *Laurie Hill*, in the role of Nurse Nancy MacIntyre. The series was canceled after only four episodes, but Marlens and Black were so impressed with DeGeneres' performance that they soon cast her in their next ABC pilot, *These Friends of Mine*, which they co-created with David S Rosenthal.

DeGeneres's comedy career became the basis of the successful sitcom *Ellen*, named *These Friends of Mine* during its first season. Teac show was popular in its first few seasons in part due to DeGeneres's style of observational humor; it was often referred to as a "female *Seinfeld*."

Ellen reached its height of popularity in February 1997, when DeGeneres came out as a lesbian on *The Oprah Winfrey Show*. That April, her character on the sitcom came out of the closet to her therapist, played by Oprah Winfrey. The coming-out episode, titled "The Puppy Episode," was one of the highest-rated episodes of the show. The series returned for a fifth season, but experienced falling ratings due to ABC's cutting back on promoting the show. It was believed that The Walt Disney Company, ABC's parent owner, had become uncomfortable with the subject matter depicted on the show now that DeGeneres' character was openly gay. In May 1998, *Ellen* was canceled. DeGeneres returned to stand-up comedy, and later re-established herself as a successful talk show host.

Ponder Points:

The LGBT community is victim to the stubborn mindsetof society. This can be overcome with a flexible mindset.Never let it hold you back. Live your dreams.

Each and every person is equal on this earth. If people try to stop you from doing what you want to do, think of them as those who cannot do anything by themselves.

Kali Muscle

"Strong People Don't Put Others Down
They Lift Them Up" – Kali Muscle

Kali Muscle is a man that tosses stereotype on its head like a rusty old dumbbell.

He is a bodybuilder, gang leader, ex-con, philosopher, actor, author, philanthropist, motivational speaker and father.

Kali Muscle was born in Oakland, California in 1975, into a neighborhood afflicted by crime and poverty.

One of three children, he was raised by his mother and stepfather, who, in his own words, treated him as the 'black sheep' of the family.

As a wide-eyed teenager, he quickly developed a love for the gym and landed his first job at 24 Hour Nautilus (now 24 Hour Fitness).

Plagued by the encroaching violence of his troubled neighborhood (he was forced to own his first gun at Elementary School), this young man from Oakland found comfort in the sweaty, metallic fumes of his local gymnasium.

Outside of the gym, Kali excelled at a multitude of sports, including wresting and track and received a football scholarship to Fresno State University, where he was a running back.

At this juncture, his life was on track.

Everything seemed to be going according to plan....

However, while Kali was in Senior Year, tragedy struck his family when his older brother was killed after 'messing around with a gun.'

His situation spiraled further into woe, when, in his second year at Fresno State, Kali ran into grave financial difficulties and soon found himself resorting to robbery to make ends meet.

He was later arrested and ended up in San Quentin State Prison, where he was to spend eleven life-changing years.

The 'Prison Work-Out'

This determined bodybuilder was not going to let a silly thing like having no weights get in the way of his muscle building goals.

So Kali Muscle devised new, innovative ways of working out, using, for example, garbage bags, water bottles and other men's bodies.

This resourcefulness continued to frustrate his prison officers, and on one occasion, he was sent to solitary confinement for refusing to eschew his passion.

The real take-away from the Kali Muscle story is his inspirational, edifying and empowering journey.

From a troubled upbringing on the streets of Oakland, via San Quentin and solitary confinement, Kali Muscle turned his life around to become a beacon of hope.

He has shown that it is possible to transcend society's shackles with tireless motivation and goodwill regardless of creed or color in order to forge a successful path.

All that's left is for me to leave you with the immortal words of the man himself:

A gang-leader does eleven years of hard time in prison and decides that he will show the world that he will defy all odds and become a great successful human being even though society had labeled him an ex-con.

Now the ex-gang leader is a successful actor, bodybuilder, philanthropist, motivational speaker, author and husband.

Now, what is your excuse for not achieving the things you want out of life?

Get off your lazy ass and go get it!

"STRONG PEOPLE DON'T PUT OTHERS DOWN

THEY LIFT THEM UP" – KALI MUSCLE

What a saying by the person who once was a gangster, had been in jail, and lived in poverty! This one is the best example of a flexible mind that is full of positivity.

Sandeep Maheshwari

"No Hill Is Tough To Climb
See You at the Top" – Sandeep Maheshwari

His family was into the Aluminium business, which collapsed and the onus was on him to earn for his family. As expected from any young guy, he started doing everything he could; right from joining a multi-level marketing company to manufacturing and marketing household products. He left no stone unturned.

It was during this phase that he discovered an interest and need beyond any formal education. Hence, instead of being a brilliant student, he opted to drop out of Kirorimal College, Delhi in the third year of B.Com. He embarked on the journey of studying yet another interesting subject. A subject called life.

Attracted by the scintillating modeling world, he started his career as a model at the age of nineteen. Witnessing the harassment and exploitation experienced by models, something in him moved. It was at this point when he decided to help countless struggling models. With a mission within, he started small. He did a two-week course in photography and became a dime-a-dozen photographer with a camera in his hand. Nothing much changed. Moving ahead with a burning desire to change the modeling world, he set up his own company, Mash Audio Visuals Pvt. Ltd., and started making portfolios.

Next, in the year 2002, he along with three friends, started a company, which closed within six months. But Sandeep's mind was still open. With the concept of "Sharing" in his heart, he summed up his entire experience in a book on marketing.

It was the year 2003. He created a world record by knocking down a juggernaut task of taking more than 10,000 shots of 122 models in just ten hours and forty-five minutes. But as expected, he didn't stop. His focus was not diluted by the glamour and temporary adulation he got. Rather, this fueled his desire to revamp the modeling world further. At the age of twenty-six, he launched ImagesBazaar. The year was 2006. Not being a massive setup, he took the job of multi-tasking. Being the counselor, tele-caller and photographer all by himself, he paved his way forward. And today, ImagesBazaar is the world's largest collection of Indian images with over a million images and more than 7000 clients across forty-fivecountries.

Sandeep has single-handedly brought a paradigm shift in the modeling world. Countless models have been successfully launched with words like exploitation and harassment side-lined to a large extent.

It was this life-changing endeavor that made him one of the most renowned entrepreneurs of India at the young age of twenty-nine. His ethics resonate philosophies such as 'Never Fear Failure' and 'Be Truthful to yourself and others.'

Points to ponder:

Dear readers, just keep your eyes on the graphs of up and downs that these people faced. Isn't it motivating you? What is stopping you? What is the biggest hurdle that is standing between you and your goal?

"Degree or age does not matter; you do what you want to do."

"Never Fear Failure."

"Be Truthful to yourself and others." - Sandeep Maheshwari

Steve Jobs

"I used to say that Apple should be the Sony of this business, but in reality, I think Apple should be the Apple of this business." – Steve Jobs

Steven Paul "Steve" Jobs (February 24, 1955 – October 5, 2011) was an American information technology entrepreneur and inventor. He was the co-founder, chairman, and chief executive officer (CEO) of Apple Inc.; CEO and majority shareholder of Pixar; a member of The Walt Disney Company's board of directors following its acquisition of Pixar; and founder, chairman, and CEO of NeXT Inc. Jobs is widely recognized as a pioneer of the microcomputer revolution of the 1970s and 1980s, along with Apple co-founder Steve Wozniak. Shortly after his death, Jobs' official biographer, Walter Isaacson, described him as a "creative entrepreneur whose passion for perfection and ferocious drive revolutionized six industries: personal computers, animated movies, music, phones, tablet computing and digital publishing."

Facts

- Steve Jobs was adopted shortly after being born.
- Jobs was, biologically, half Arab. His biological father was Syrian and his mother was American.
- Jobs' biological parents had one mandate–that Jobs be adopted by two college-educated people. The biological parents found out that neither Clara nor Paul Jobs had ever graduated from college, but the adoption went through when it was promised that Steve Jobs would receive a university education (funny considering that Jobs went on to become a college dropout).
- Jobs and Apple co-founder Steve Wozniak met in high school–Wozniak was 18 and Jobs was just 13.
- Jobs was a pescetarian, meaning he ate no meat except for fish.
- He was an official college dropout, but continued his education by informally auditing classes.
- One class Jobs audited was a calligraphy course, which he says was instrumental in the future Apple products' attention to typography and font.
- While unofficially attending classes, Jobs struggled to get by. He slept on his friends' dorm room floors,

returned Coke bottles for money and survived off free meals from the local Hare Krishna temple.

- He had a pretty low GPA– just 2.65. Jobs admitted he never enjoyed school structure and preferred to learn in unconventional ways.
- He spent seven months traveling around India, experimenting with psychedelic drugs and eventually adopting the practices of Zen Buddhism.
- Jobs has called experimenting with LSD as "one of the two or three most important things I have done in my life."
- Jobs stole from partner and co-founder of Apple Steve Wozniak. When the pair first created the Breakout game for Atari, they planned on splitting the pay 50-50. Although Atari gave Jobs $5,000 for the game, Jobs told Wozniak they got $700, leaving Wozniak to take home $350 while Jobs pocketed the other $4,650.
- Jobs was moved to the night shift when working at Atari due to complaints about his hygiene. He rarely showered and would walk around barefoot in the Atari offices.
- There was actually a third founder of Apple–Ronald Wayne, who even designed Apple's first logo. Wayne sold his 10 percent stake just two weeks after partnering with Jobs and Wozniak for only $800 (talk about regrets).
- The original Apple I computer was priced at $666.66. Don't worry, there was no devil worshipping going on–Jobs and Wozniak just wanted the Apple I to cost one-third more than wholesale ($500).

- Jobs was pushed out of his own company in 1985. Despite the fallout, he later recognized the coup as a blessing in disguise, as it gave him a chance to experiment creatively and purchase an animation studio, which would later be known as Pixar. Eventually he rejoined Apple as CEO in 1997 (and revitalized the failing company).
- Shortly after being shooed out of Apple, Jobs applied to fly on the Space Shuttle as a civilian astronaut (he was rejected) and even considered starting a computer company in the Soviet Union.
- Jobs had an illegitimate child, Lisa Brennan, when he was 23, whose paternity he denied for years. Lisa's mother had to use welfare checks to raise her child. Eventually, Jobs did accept Lisa as his legitimate child, and she changed her name to Lisa Brennan-Jobs.
- Despite initially denying paternity, around the time Lisa was born, Jobs named a new Apple computer the Apple Lisa (although Jobs claimed it simply stood for Local Integrated Software Architecture).
- While at Apple, Jobs always kept his annual salary at $1. Don't worry, with 5.5 million shares of Apple stock and as the majority shareholder of Disney stock (from selling Pixar); he wasn't *quite* what you'd call a starving artist.
- Jobs ended up connecting later in life with his biological sister, Mona Simpson, whom he grew very close with. Both were naturally artistic and shared much in common.

- The movie *Anywhere but Here* is based on a book written by Jobs's sister, Mona Simpson. The movie is dedicated to Jobs.
- Jobs wasno philanthropist. In fact, in Apple's early days, he cut the company's philanthropic programs, saying they would return when the company was more profitable. Despite Apple's enormous success, the charitable programs were never reinstated.
- Jobs had an entire team devoted to packaging who studied the experience of opening a box to learn how to achieve the excitement and emotional response that is now common with Apple products.
- A well-known egomaniac, Jobs was infamous for being difficult and demanding. In 1993, he held a spot on *Fortune*'s list of America's Toughest Bosses.
- Jobs were not always friendly with journalists and the media, wanting to retain total control of Apple's impression on the public. Apple even sued teenager Nicholas Ciarelli for his Think Secret blog, where he revealed rumors and secret details about upcoming Apple products.
- Jobs is listed as either primary inventor or co-inventor for 346 United States patents related to a range of technologies, with most of the patents being for design.
- Jobs had romantic relationships with Joan Baez and Diane Keaton.
- Apple co-founder Steve Wozniak notes that Jobs never learned how to code.

- Bill Clinton once invited Jobs to spend the night sleeping in the Lincoln bedroom of the White House.
- Apple has been ranked No. 1 on *Fortune*'s list of America's most admired companies.
- Jobs harbored an intense dislike for PCs, and is quoted as saying to one friend, "I'd rather sell dog shit than PCs."
- He never put license plates on his silver Mercedes (despite driving it constantly). How did he do it? California has a rule that a car owner has six months to put plates on a new car. Jobs just changed cars (to the identical model) every six months, allowing him to drive without plates.
- Jobs often parked in spots reserved for the handicapped.
- Jobs originally did not want to offer his products in white, but he was swayed after being introduced to the "moon gray" shade. Pretty surprising considering the iconic clean, white look of Apple products today.
- Jobs actually served as a mentor for Google founders Sergey Brin and Larry Page, even sharing some of his advisers with the Google duo.
- Jobs was furious when Google created its Android devices, entering as an Apple competitor in the phone market.
- Jobs was found to have pancreatic cancer in 2003, but rather than taking the doctor-recommended path of immediate operation, Jobs subscribed to an alternative-medicine regimen, including a vegan diet,

acupuncture, and herbal remedies, even consulting a psychic.

- After nine months, Jobs gave in and underwent surgery. Many consider the delay a major factor in his eventual decline.
- Apple, Microsoft and Disney properties (including Disneyland and Disney World) flew their flags at half-staff when Jobs died.
- His last words on his deathbed were, "Oh wow, oh wow, oh wow," while gazing over his family's shoulders.
- Tim Cook revealed in a 2014 interview that Jobs's main office and nameplate are still as they were in 2011, when Jobs passed away.
- Sunday, October 16, 2011, was declared Steve Jobs Day by the governor of California, Jerry Brown.

Ingvar Kamprad

"Only those who are asleep make no mistake" - Ingvar Kamprad

Ingvar Feodor Kamprad (born 30 March, 1926) is a Swedish business magnate. He is the founder of IKEA, a Swedish retail company specializing in furniture.

Kamprad began to develop a business as a young boy, selling matches to neighbors from his bicycle. He found that he could buy matches in bulk very cheaply from Stockholm, sell them individually at a low price and still make a good profit. From matches, he expanded to selling fish, Christmas tree decorations, seeds, and later, ballpoint pens and pencils. When Kamprad was 17, his father gave him a cash reward for succeeding in his studies despite being dyslexic.

Net worth 3.3 billion USD

Key Points:

Be a Visionary. The one who visualizes his goal, can achieve it.

Walt Disney

"If you can dream it, you can do it." – Walt Disney

Walter Elias "Walt" Disney (December 5, 1901 – December 15, 1966) was an American entrepreneur, animator, voice actor and film producer. A pioneer of the American animation industry, he introduced several developments in the production of cartoons. As a film producer he received 22 Academy Awards from 59 nominations and has won more individual Oscars than anyone else. He was presented with two Golden Globe Special Achievement Awards and one Emmy Award, among other honors. Several of his films are included in the National Film Registry by the Library of Congress.

In 1917, Elias bought stock in a Chicago jelly producer, the O-Zell Company, and moved back to the city with his family. Disney enrolled at McKinley High School and became the cartoonist of the school newspaper, drawing patriotic pictures about World War I; he also took night courses at the Chicago Academy of Fine Arts. In mid-1918, Disney attempted to join the United States Army to fight against the Germans, but he was rejected for being too young. After forging the date of birth on his birth certificate, he joined the Red Cross in September 1918 as an ambulance driver. He was shipped to France but arrived in November, after the armistice. He drew cartoons on the side of his ambulance for decoration and had some of his work published in the army newspaper *Stars and Stripes*. Disney returned to Kansas City in October 1919, where he worked as an apprentice artist at the Pesmen-Rubin Commercial Art Studio. There, he drew commercial illustrations for advertising, theater programs and catalogs. He also befriended fellow artist UbIwerks.

Ponder points:

Know your strengths.

Azim Premji

"If people are not laughing at your goals, your goals are too small." – Azim Premji

Azim Hashim Premji (born 24 July, 1945) is an Indian business tycoon, investor and philanthropist, who is the chairman of Wipro Limited, informally known as the Czar of the Indian

IT Industry. He was responsible for guiding Wipro through four decades of diversification and growth to finally emerge as one of the global leaders in the Software Industry. In 2010, he was voted as one among the twenty most powerful men in the world by *Asia Week*. He has twice been listed among the 100 most influential people by TIME Magazine, once in 2004 and more recently in 2011. Premji owns 73% of Wipro and also owns a private equity fund, Premji Invest, which manages his $2 billion worth of personal portfolio. In 2013, he e away 25% of his personal wealth to charity and has also pledged to give away the rest of the 25% in the next 5 years.

In 1945, Muhammed Hashim Premji incorporated Western Indian Vegetable Products Ltd., based in Amalner, a small town in the Jalgaon district of Maharashtra. It used to manufacture cooking oil under the brand name Sunflower Vanaspati, and a laundry soap called 787, a by product of oil manufacture. In 1966, on the news of his father's death, the then 21-year-old Azim Premji returned home from Stanford University, where he was studying engineering, to take charge of Wipro. The company, which was called Western Indian Vegetable Products at the time, dealt in hydrogenated oil manufacturing, but Azim Premji later diversified the company to bakery fats, ethnic ingredient-based toiletries, hair care soaps, baby toiletries, lighting products and hydraulic cylinders. In the 1980s, the young entrepreneur, recognizing the importance of the emerging IT field, took advantage of the vacuum left behind by the expulsion of IBM from India, changed the company name to *Wipro* and entered the high-technology sector by manufacturing minicomputers under technological collaboration with an American company Sentinel Computer Corporation. Thereafter, Premji made a focused shift from soaps to software.

Key Points:

- Change and innovation is what leads to success in business.
- A flexible mindset is the reason for his enormous wealth

Chris Dawson

telegraph.co.uk Article

The self-made retail billionaire who can't read or write

Chris Dawson can't read or write. However, that doesn't stop the billionaire founder of The Range from communicating with his army of employees – he simply subjects them to phone calls at dawn.

"If I've got a good idea, even if it's at three o'clock in the morning I just can't contain it, I have got to tell someone," Dawson says.

The 64-year-old, who has turned The Range into a booming chain of retail park shops selling everything

from lawn-mowers and hammocks to artists' sketch-pads, believes in squeezing the most out of his day.

Chris Dawson (born 15 February, 1952) is a British businessman; founder, owner and CEO of the British retail chain The Range.

Dawson was born in Plymouth, Devonto a market trader. He attended Hooe Primary School and then Plymstock Secondary School. Dawson attended school irregularly, struggled with dyslexia and left school at the age of fifteen with limited qualifications.

Dawson started as a market trader in Plymouth. He sold seafood from the back of a van with his father and later started his own venture selling perfume and jewelry from a suitcase.

Dawson started CDS Superstores (Chris Dawson Superstores) in 1989, and opened an outlet store in Sugar Mill Business Park in Plymouth called The Range Home, Garden & Leisure. The store sold toys, homewares, DIY equipment and jewelry.

A 'The Range Home, Garden & Leisure' brand store was opened in Cardiff in February 2000; Dawson later bought the business park where this store sits. The Range was featured in The Sunday Times Top Track 250 companies from 2003 to 2012, once ranking at number 48. In 2015, the retail chain had about 100 stores, all of which were owned directly by Dawson.

Dawson's CDS Superstores International Company started a subsidiary, CDS Group Services, a shop fitting company that has clients such as Lego, Lush Cosmetics, Levi's Jeans and sister company The Range. CDS Group Services was listed in twelfth place in the Real Business Hot 100 Companies in 2012.

Dawson was an ambassador for the *Channel 4 Jobs Report* in 2012, named the Ernst & Young Overall Entrepreneur of the

Year in 2011 and in the same year advised the Prime Minister David Cameron on issues facing growing businesses. In 2012, he was interviewed by Justin Leigh on BBC Radio Devon.

In 2013, Dawson's businesses had an estimated worth of 585 million pounds. He has established several other companies involved in property, dry cleaning, manufacturing and waste management services.

In April 2015, the *Sunday Times'* Rich List reported that his net worth was £1.65 billion.

Key Points:

- Even if the odds are against you, and there is no one to support you, believe in yourself.
- If a person with dyslexia, who cannot read or write, can become a billionaire by himself, why can't we?
- "Formal education will make you a living;
  Self-education will make you a fortune." – Jim Rohn

Mayer Amschel Rothschild

Known to many as the pioneers of international banking, the Rothschild dynasty is believed to be the wealthiest family in the history of the world. According to some estimates, the Rothschild family controls assets worth more than $350 billion when each of their personal fortunes is combined.

Mayer Amschel Rothschild (23 February 1744 - 19 September 1812), was a German Jewish banker and the founder of the Rothschild banking dynasty, which is believed to have become the wealthiest family in human history. Referred to as the "founding father of international finance," Rothschild was ranked seventh on the *Forbes* magazine list of “The Twenty Most Influential Businessmen of All Time” in 2005.

The Rothschild’s story of power and riches began with the humble beginnings of its founder, Mayer Rothschild. Born in 1744, Mayer Rothschild was raised in a Jewish ghetto in Frankfurt, Germany. During that era, Jews were legally required to live in small communities that were distant from Christians. They were also not allowed to leave their villages on Christian holidays, Sundays or at night.

As a child, Rothschild lived in a full house with about thirty other family members. Rothschild learned about the business world at an early age–his father, Amschel Moses Rothschild, traded coins, silk and other commodities for a living. One of Amschel Rothschild’s clients was the Prince of Hesse.

Mayer Rothschild became an orphan at the age of twelve following the death of his mother. His father had died from smallpox the year before. Before their passing, Rothschild’s parents wanted their son to study Jewish teaching to become a Rabbi. However, he decided to take on an apprenticeship with a banking firm in Hanover, Germany shortly after turning thirteen. The firm was operated by Court Jews who furnished credit to European royalty. During his time there, Rothschild learned the ins and outs of banking and foreign trade

Quote by Heinrich Heine on Rothschild:

“Money is the god of our time, and Rothschild is his prophet” – Heinrich Heine

Giorgio Armani

"Elegance is about being noticed; It's about being remembered" – Gorgio Armani

Designer Giorgio Armani was born on July 11, 1934, in Piacenza, Italy. With his body-conscious yet understated clothing, Giorgio Armani has become one of the most popular names in fashion. He first launched his business empire in the mid-1970s, and it has grown substantially over the years. The Armani brand now includes makeup, housewares, books and hotels.

The son of a shipping manager, Armani grew up in a small town outside of Milan. It was a difficult time in Italian history. Giorgio and his two siblings– older brother Sergio and younger sister Rosanna – experienced the hardships of World War II first-hand. Some of his friends were killed during Allied bombings. "We were poor and life was tough," he explained to *Harper's Bazaar.* "The cinema in Milan was a refuge—a palace of dreams—and the movie stars seemed so glamorous. I fell in love with the idealized beauty of Hollywood stars."

At an early age, Armani developed an interest in anatomy, making "dolls out of mud with a coffee bean hidden inside," he explained to the *Guardian.* His fascination with the human form led to two years of medical study at the University of Piacenza. Taking a break from school, Armani had to complete his required military service. He soon got his first taste of fashion. "I was doing my military service and I had twenty days off on vacation in Milan," he explained to *Time* magazine. Through a friend, he got a job at a department store. "I started assisting the photographer, designing the windows and things."

After completing his military service, Armani dropped out of university and went to work at La Rinascente, a famous Milan department store. He then joined the staff of Nino Cerruti as a designer. With the encouragement of his friend Sergio Galeotti, Armani started to do freelance design work for other companies as well.

Armani and Galeotti became business partners, founding Giorgio Armani S.p.A. in July 1975. The company's first collection—a men's clothing line—debuted that year. Armani launched a women's collection the following year, which received a warm reception. His clothes were revolutionary at the time, introducing a more natural fit and using a subtle color palette. "My vision was clear: I believed in getting rid of the artifice of clothing. I believed in neutral colors," he later told *WWD*.

Despite his great success, Armani remains modest about his efforts. "I like the idea of having built this beautiful empire, but I still like to think of myself as the stable boy," he told *WWD*. Several family members work for him in this vast enterprise. His sister Rosanna works at Armani as do two of his nieces, Silvana and Roberta.

With more than three decades in the business, Armani has enjoyed longevity as a designer experienced by few others. Some compare him to such fashion greats as Coco Chanel and Yves Saint Laurent. In his 70s, Armani stands as one of fashion's most distinguished leaders. He seems "almost presidential—wise, serene and comfortable in his role now as the reigning eminence of Milan fashion," wrote a journalist for *The New York Times*.

Points to Note:

Being down to earth is the quality seen in many billionaires.

Michael Dell

"You don't have to be genius or a visionaryor even a college graduate to be successful. You just need a framework and a dream." – Micheal dell

Michael Saul Dell (born February 23, 1965) is an American business magnate, investor, philanthropist and author. He is the founder and CEO of Dell Inc., one of the world's leading sellers of personal computers (PCs). He was ranked the 41st richest person in the world on 2012 Forbes list of billionaires, with a net worth of US$22.4 billion as of December 2014.

In 2011, his 243.35 million shares of Dell stock were worth $3.5 billion, giving him 12% ownership of the company. His remaining wealth of roughly $10 billion is invested in other companies and is managed by a firm whose name, MSD Capital, incorporates Dell's initials. On January 5, 2013 it was announced that Michael Dell had bid to take Dell Inc. private for $24.4 billion in the biggest management since the Great Recession. Dell Inc. officially went private on October 29, 2013.

While a freshman pre-med student at the University of Texas, Dell started an informal business putting together and selling upgrade kits for personal computers in Room 2713 of the Dobie Center residential building. He then applied for a vendor license to bid on contracts for the State of Texas, winning bids by not having the overhead of a computer store.

In January 1984, Dell banked on his conviction that the potential cost savings of a manufacturer selling PCs directly had enormous advantages over the conventional indirect retail channel. In January 1984, Dell registered his company as "PC's Limited." Operating out of a condominium, the business sold between $50,000 and $80,000 in upgraded PCs, kits, and add-on components. In May, Dell incorporated the company as "Dell Computer Corporation" and relocated it to a business center in North Austin. The company employed a few order takers, a few more people to fulfill them, and, as Dell recalled, a manufacturing staff "consisting of three guys with screwdrivers sitting at six-foot tables." The venture's capitalization cost was $1,000.

In 1992, aged 27, he became the youngest CEO of a company ranked in *Fortune* magazine's list of the top 500 corporations. In 1996, Dell started selling computers over the Web, the same year his company launched its first servers. Dell Inc. soon reported about $1 million in sales per day from dell.com. In the first quarter of 2001, Dell Inc. reached a world market share of 12.8 percent, passing Compaq to become the world's largest PC maker. The metric marked the first time the rankings had shifted over the previous seven years. The company's combined shipments of desktops, notebooks and servers grew 34.3 percent worldwide and 30.7 percent in the United States at a time when competitor's sales were shrinking.

In 1998, Dell founded MSD Capital L.P. to manage his family's investments. Investment activities include publicly traded securities, private equity activities, and real estate. The firm employs 80 people and has offices in New York, Santa Monica and London. Dell himself is not involved in day-to-day operations. On March 4, 2004, Dell stepped down as CEO, but stayed as chairman of Dell Inc.'s board, while Kevin Rollins, then president and COO, became president and CEO. On January 31, 2007, Dell returned as CEO at the request of the board, succeeding Rollins.

Points:

THERE IS NO BETTER CATALYST TO SUCCESS THAN CURIOSITY.

Be Curious.

Mimi & Alex Ikonn

> *"When I started making money, I stopped thinking about myself" - Alex Ikonn*

They are famous YouTube celebrities and the owners of successful luxury brand Luxy Hairs.

They share their stories and motivate people on their YouTube channel.

Please make sure you visit Mimi & Alex Ikonn's YouTube channels, 'Mimi Ikonn' and 'Alex Ikonn,' where you will get to know exciting things about their lives and their travel experiences.

Alex and Mimi used to work in a bank and made a life-changing decision of starting a business. If I tell you everything, I may ruin the true essence and thrill of their story so please visit their channel.

Formula for Success

Failure + Motivation + Research + Hard Work + Attitude + Introspection = Success

Consider If

A B C D E F G H I J K L M N O P Q R S T U V W X Y Z

=

1 2 3 4 5 6 7 8 9 10 11 12 13 14 15 16 17 18 19 20 21 22 23 24 25 26

Then,

K N O W L E D G E

11 + 14 + 15 + 23 + 12 + 5 + 4 + 7 + 5 = 96%

H A R D W O R K

8 + 1 + 18 + 4 + 23 + 15 + 18 + 11 = 98%

But

A T T I T U D E

1 + 20 + 20 + 9 + 20 + 21 + 45 = 100%

Let's talk about Attitude with a flexible mindset. Attitude is nothing but the way we look at a situation, good or bad.

Sometimes, we misunderstand failure. They can be blessings in disguise, and sometimes success can be a curse in disguise.

Their Stories in Brief

1. Bill Gates – Failed at his first business venture, Traf-O-Dataat the age of seventeen and then went on to co-found one of the biggest companies of the century. Is the richest person in the world.
2. Dhirubhai Ambani – Failed in 10th grade. Worked in a petrol station and went on to become the biggest and smartest businessman in history.
3. Dr Subhash Chandra - 10th grade dropout who is the founder of one of the first TV channels, Zee TV, in India and is a great philanthropist.
4. Sir Richard Branson – School dropout who had dyslexia.He founded theVirgin Group.
5. Mahashay Dharampal Gulati – A person known to every household in India through his brand name MDH masala. Started his journey from the middle of nowhere.
6. Henry Ford - Founded two automotive companies that failed before he was able to gain success with the Ford Motor Company. One of the richest persons ever to live on Earth.
7. Swami Ramdev Baba – Suffered paralysis at a very young age. He cured his own illness and went on to cure people across the globe. His journey has been epic.

8. Oprah Winfrey– Hailed as the "**Queen of Daytime Talk TV**," Winfrey was fired from her news reporter gig at a Baltimore news station. Oprah went on to build a successful following from her daytime talk show "The Oprah Winfrey Show."
9. Ellen DeGeneres- "It's failure that gives you the proper perspective on success." Ellen DeGeneres, *Seriously… I'm Kidding*

Ellen was fired for her sexual preference. She went on to become the most-loved talk show host and a millionaire.

Seriously… I'm Kidding is her book; please read it.

10. Kali Muscle – Was in jail at a very young age for seven years and used the experience to become a positive motivation speaker, an actor, a businessman, and a millionaire.
11. Sandeep Maheshwari – College dropout who created a world record by taking more than 10,000 shots of 122 models in just 10 hours and 45 minutes.
12. Steve Jobs– Was fired from **Apple Computers**, the very company that he was responsible for making the success it is today. When Jobs was fired from Apple, he was quoted having said,"I didn't see it then, but it turned out that **getting fired from Apple was the best thing that could have ever happened to me**. The heaviness of being successful was replaced by the lightness of being a beginner again, less sure about everything. **It freed me** to enter one of the most creative periods of my life."

13. **Ingvar Kamprad – Founder of IKEA. Started his business at a very young age.**
14. **Walt Disney** -Walt Disney is the businessman behind the very successful theme park **Walt Disney World.** Walt Disney was reportedly fired by a newspaper editor for not having good ideas and for having no imagination.
15. Azim Premji – Turned a small business into a massive empire.
16. Chris Dawson – Can't read or write but is a self-made billionaire.
17. **Mayer Amschel Rothschild** - "Money Is The God Of Our Time, And Rothschild Is His Prophet" – Heinrich Heine, you can guess who he was.
18. **Giorgio Armani** - Department-store window dresser who became a fashion king.
19. **Michael Dell – A dropout who went on** to hold the reins of a maverick venture and achieved the unique distinction of being the computer industry's longest-tenured CEO.
20. Mimi & Alex Ikonn – A dropout and a bank employee who became motivational speakers and millionaires.

"BE THE CHANGE YOU WANT TO SEE IN THE WORLD" - M K GANDHI

Let's begin....

Conclusion

And now, I wish to share a wonderful story. Once, in a small village, lived a young boy called Shyam Sunder. He was very affectionate towards his villagers who also showered him with affection. However, whenever he attended social gatherings, he would hear a lot of complaints from them about all the evils that prevailed in the society.

He also observed that this affected the younger generation negatively. They lost their enthusiasm and positivity. Shyam made up his mind to motivate the people and bring some change in their mindsets. He decided to invite a sage to the village.

He discussed the problem with Ramji sadhu, who was invited to give a religious seminar. This was the first major event in the village, so all the villagers were very keen to hear him.

Some prodigious arrangements were made at the old village temple.

The scholarly sadhu arrived, and he was received with a cordial welcome. Ramji sadhu expressed his desire to look around the village before he began the religious discourse. Arrangements were soon made; a beautiful horse chariot was made ready for the swamiji's tour in the village. Shyam was very happy to see the enthusiasm on the faces of his beloved villagers. He was sure that the swamiji would be able to bring positivity back in the atmosphere of his village.

To the surprise of the villagers, swamiji refused to ride on the chariot and preferred to walk. The procession began. They first visited the old monuments in the village and then the beautiful school surroundings. Suddenly, swamiji pointed at a filthy place where the surroundings were not so pleasant. He went there and sat under a tree. He took a deep breath. The villagers were astonished.

Swamiji said, “I can sense the aroma of some delicious Prasad being cooked.”

One of the curious villagers asked,“Swamiji, the place where prasad is getting cooked is quite far and this place is so filthy with a bad stench. How is it possible for you to sense the smell of Prasad?”

With a beautiful and calm smile, swamiji replied, “It’s just the matter of choice. Nature is full of good and evil. It depends on what we choose to look at. We have been blessed with the ability to differentiate between good and bad, so a wise person will always ignore the filthy part and will only take in the beauty and the goodness. Only by doing so, the aura of positivity will spread and the disgusting smell of evil and its negativity will vanish.”

The villagers understood the teachings of the sage.

No matter how rigid the norms of the society maybe; no matter how unfavorable the situation may seem; if you have a positive attitude, no one can stop you from becoming successful. All our heroes mentioned above faced various tough situations but instead of losing hope they decided to spread love and a helping hand to the needy.

So dear ones, live life to the fullest. Don’t get disheartened by the unconventional situation or people that you come across in your journey towards success. Be in an incognito mode, i.e., never save any negative situation in your mind and heart.

Believe that one day, your circumstances will change and that you will succeed in your life. After innumerable attempts, people tend to give up and forget the fact that they were very close to reaching their goal.

We all may have heard about the people listed in this book, but we tend to forget them in the hustle and bustle of everyday life. This book is like a daily manual that will always be around you and will keep you motivated.

You will find that people in this book have different origins, belong to different age groups and centuries and have different ways of doing business. However, you will notice that each and every one of them came from a very humble background, but pushed ahead with confidence.

No matter what your problem is, there is always a way out. You just need to collect the remnants of your soul, piece it together and fight for what you believe in.

And let me tell you that it will hurt, but you cannot afford to lose as losing is not an option…losing is never an option.

I remember a quote by Bruce lee:

"Defeat is a state of mind; no one is ever defeated until defeat has been accepted as a reality."

Believe me, you are not alone in this situation.

Undesirable situations may seem to be against you. They may bring you down to your feet, but if you stand tall and face them bravely, they will flee like a coward.

I chose to show twenty business persons because they have always fascinated me. Their way of doing business and their way of living life are absolutely the same.

This doesn't mean I consider money as the ultimate scale for success.

Success is what makes you happy.

For example: Dr Prakash Baba Amte spent his entire life uplifting downtrodden people and taking care of impaired animals. That's a life worth living!

History is proof that you need just 3P's for success:

- Patience
- Perseverance
- Perspiration
- I wish you lots of good luck and prosperity. Keep spreading love and enjoy the beauty of positivity in the world. Let all negativity vanish by always speaking good words, and never backbite anyone. As a result, you will be filled with the glory of positivity and will attract good luck towards you.

Don't sweat the small stuff. Have a flexible mindset.

And as Ellen says, "Be kind to one another."

And keep waiting for *Mindset,* my next book that is coming soon....

References

1. https://en.wikipedia.org/wiki/Bill_Gates
2. http://thepurposeisprofit.com/2015/07/28/bill-gates-steve-jobs-risk-failure-and-success/
3. http://www.indiatimes.com/lifestyle/self/9-indian-failures-who-became-inspirational-success-stories-227984.html
4. http://brainprick.com/dhirubhai-ambani-a-real-rags-to-riches-story/
5. http://www.2knowmyself.com/Dhirubhai_ambani_success_story
6. https://en.wikipedia.org/wiki/Dhirubhai_Ambani
7. https://en.wikipedia.org/wiki/Subhash_Chandra
8. http://www.esselgroup.com/search.html?keyword=Dr+Subhash+Chandra&x=0&y=0
9. http://zeenews.india.com/business/news/companies/essel-group-chairman-dr-subhash-chandra-to-launch-his-autobiography-today_1847137.html
10. https://twitter.com/subhashchandra/status/667903468544376832
11. http://attitudes4innovation.com/7-success-quotes-from-richard-branson/

12. https://www.youtube.com/watch?v=vxHnVnBXf2k
13. https://www.youtube.com/watch?v=dG4Fi5KYzpc
14. http://www.fastcompany.com/3002809/be-henry-ford-apprentice-yourself-failure
15. https://en.wikipedia.org/wiki/Ellen_DeGeneres
16. http://www.gym-talk.com/kali-muscle/
17. http://kalimuscle.com/kalis-blog/about-kali/
18. https://en.wikipedia.org/wiki/Richard_Branson
19. https://en.wikipedia.org/wiki/Mahashian_Di_Hatti
20. http://blog.uncollege.org/overcoming-failure-the-pereseverance-of-henry-ford
21. https://en.wikipedia.org/wiki/Henry_Ford
22. https://en.wikipedia.org/wiki/Ramdev
23. http://www.realityviews.in/2011/06/short-biography-of-baba-ramdev-history.html
24. https://en.wikipedia.org/wiki/Oprah_Winfrey
25. http://www.oprah.com/pressroom/Oprah-Winfreys-Official-Biography/6
26. http://www.sandeepmaheshwari.com/
27. http://allaboutstevejobs.com/sayings/stevejobsquotes.php
28. http://www.inc.com/larry-kim/43-surprising-facts-about-steve-jobs.html
29. https://sweden.se/business/ingvar-kamprad-founder-of-ikea/
30. https://en.wikipedia.org/wiki/Ingvar_Kamprad
31. https://en.wikipedia.org/wiki/Walt_Disney
32. http://www.azimpremjifoundation.org/Our_Vision

33. https://en.wikipedia.org/wiki/Azim_Premji
34. https://en.wikipedia.org/wiki/Jay_Van_Andel
35. http://www.ratbags.com/rsoles/comment/vanandel.pdf
36. https://en.wikipedia.org/wiki/Micky_Jagtiani
37. http://www.telegraph.co.uk/business/2016/04/10/monday-interview-chris-dawson--the-billionaire-founder-of-the-ra/
38. https://en.wikipedia.org/wiki/Chris_Dawson_(businessman)
39. https://en.wikipedia.org/wiki/Mayer_Amschel_Rothschild
40. http://www.investopedia.com/articles/investing/111915/how-rothschild-family-created-their-wealth.asp
41. http://www.biography.com/people/giorgio-armani-9188652#early-life
42. https://en.wikipedia.org/wiki/Giorgio_Armani
43. https://en.wikipedia.org/wiki/Michael_Dell
44. https://en.wikipedia.org/wiki/Ralph_Lauren
45. http://small-bizsense.com/10-famous-entrepreneurs-who-failed-in-business-before-becoming-successful/
46. http://www.success.com/blog/how-giorgio-armani-got-his-career-into-gear
47. https://www.entrepreneur.com/article/197566

www.ingramcontent.com/pod-product-compliance
Lightning Source LLC
LaVergne TN
LVHW090317160826
845684LV00001B/3

* 9 7 9 8 8 9 4 9 8 6 6 8 5 *